Liberalism Debunked
By Parker Bono

Also By Parker Bono

The Stance To Lead

The Stance To Get Elected

The Truth About The Fed

*As always,
I dedicate this book to the American
people and those who fight and fought
for me and my rights.*

Contents

Introduction

Liberalism Debunked is a book that debunks policies typically believed by those on the left. It explains why the policy or idea is bad, and what really should be the case. From economic ideas to social ideas, this book has it all.

The author of this book, Parker Bono, has written three other books, and is a mere 13 years old. Parker put lots of time and effort into this book, and Parker hopes you enjoy it.

Chapter One
Minimum Wage

"To anger a conservative, lie to him. To anger a liberal, tell him the truth." -Theodore Roosevelt

---

Liberals, or the vast majority of them at least, want an increased minimum wage. Unfortunately, most people don't know the consequences that occur when this happens. Entry level jobs, or minimum wage jobs, are the first step on the employment ladder. These jobs also typically teach people, or employees, important skills that usually aren't learned in school such as providing good customer experience, delivering results, learning how to manage money, and how to work on a team.

Well, when the government begins raising pay rates, bad things happen. Here's an example. The industry with the most minimum wage salary workers is the restaurant industry. The profit margin in restaurants is extremely low, companies make a mere $5 for every $100 in sales. One current proposal is to raise the minimum wage for restaurant workers by about 200%.

Now, what do you believe will happen to the employee at the restaurant? Well, he would either be out of work, which hurts the economy and himself, or, to balance out the loss of profit, companies will raise prices, which hurts buyers of the products. You however can't raise prices too much as that takes away customers, so most of the time, companies will either fire employees or replace them with self service or automated service providers. Companies may also cut hours worked each week by employees. According to the Congressional Budget Office, raising the federal minimum wage to $10.10 from $7.25 would cost over 500,000 jobs in the first year alone. That is obviously not good, but it gets worse for the proposed $15 federal minimum wage. Enacting a $15 minimum wage would cause the hourly cost of a full-time employee to rise to $18.61, when including payroll taxes, and the dreaded individual mandate. Raising the minimum wage to $15 would also result in the loss of approximately 6,600,000 employees, according to the Congressional Budget Office's formula.

So, with all that being said, what is the right minimum wage you may be asking? Well, the correct answer is $0. There should be no minimum wage in America. Now, this is how it should be, but that doesn't mean that it ever will be. I am a compromiser, I am willing to compromise, and I will make the deal workout well for whatever side is best. In this case I want the deal to workout well for Americans, the economy, the employees, and the employers.

The best idea is to leave the federal minimum wage alone. This would be the likely proposition I would endorse as a compromise if necessary, but as I said before, the best thing for everyone is the elimination of the minimum wage.

The right minimum wage is $0.00. This was the headline on the New York Times in 1987. They wrote "There's a virtual consensus among economists that the minimum wage is an idea whose time has passed." This consensus was made because they realized that a minimum wage absolutely does not guarantee jobs. Instead, it guarantees that those who have jobs will get paid at least a certain amount, and like

I said earlier, this will lead to two things: higher unemployment rates and higher prices.

I can show you this best by asking you a question: what is a wage? A wage is, to put it simply, the cost of labor. Now, what do you think happens if the cost of labor goes up not because individuals are becoming more productive or companies are trying to hold on to valuable employees, but merely because the government says so? Well, what will happen is known as an adjustment. Employers will either use less employees or shorten the amount of hours worked by employees, as I stated earlier. They will also raise prices for their products or services. This is all an unwanted effect.

Corporations don't do this because they are greedy, they do it since they value their $15 per hour more than they do the value of one's work per hour. Some people work better or worse than others, it's how it works. If the minimum wage truly worked, why not make it $100 per hour, or just raise the minimum wage in all the poor countries in the world? The answer is because it doesn't work the way liberals dream that it will.

There also is one more effect that I haven't really talked about yet. As a result of a higher minimum wage, businesses will hire less employees, and they will target those with the least experience first. These people are typically the very millennials in college or high school whining about a salary increase themselves, and they are the ones that will be hurt the most. Let's say that you never had a job before and we're trying to get one. You would be applying for a minimum wage job. Now, let's say there is no minimum and that your work is worth $7 per hour. You and your employer agree to the salary, and now you have a job. But instead, let's say that the minimum wage is $10 per hour, but your work is still worth just $7 per hour. Well, you would be unemployed, even if you were willing to work for $7 per hour. Even the liberal economist Paul Samuelson agrees with this. To quote Paul "What good does it do a black youth to know that an employer must pay him a minimum wage if the fact that he must be paid this wage keeps him from getting a job?"

Also, the young person in our situation above doesn't just lose a salary, they also lose essential experience that will help them get a better job in the future, as I stated earlier.

Studies suggest that the unemployment rate, in large cities, of teens who don't have a high school diploma is 50%. Inflating these people out of the workforce does nothing but harm. Teens who don't end up finding jobs will typically find trouble.

Those who advocate for a higher minimum wage claim that the fact some people will be priced out of the market (6,600,000 to be exact) is outweighed by the fact that those who keep their minimum wage jobs will get an increased wage. This however doesn't mean that people would be better off. The government can force businesses to pay more money per hour, but they can not force businesses to pay more money each week. Corporations will just cut the amount of hours worked per week. According to the Los Angles Times, after Connecticut raised it's minimum wage from $8.70 to $10,10, many employees got their hours worked cut. One worker in the particular interview got their weekly hours cut from 35 to 27. This means that that minimum wage increase actually ended up earning that person less money than before.

You see, under a system with no minimum wage, corporations don't get all the control, it's a mutual agreement, and the value of your work would vary, as would your salary. If people opened up their minds, they would see that the elimination of the minimum wage is the best thing for us, but like I said before, right now it won't happen. My compromise I would offer liberals would be to leave it untouched at the federal level, and if certain states change their minimum wage, we will allow the free market to determine the economy of that state. I of course would vastly prefer that this isn't the case, but this is the best alternative you will get from me. You would be stupid not to vote for someone who wants to end the minimum wage as that is what will be best for everyone as a whole, but unless we wake people up, they won't vote for that person.

Chapter Two
Taxes

"A man in debt is so far a slave."
-Ralph Waldo Emerson

Before I say anything in this chapter, let me introduce you to one of the most important things in taxes: the laffer curve. This concept states the most important things people must know about taxes: how much money the government can get through taxation and the right level of taxation.

The laffer curve has many different points, depending on the rate of taxation. In the beginning, the line goes up, but later on, it goes down. This means there is a hump on this graph. Now, whenever you pass the hump or peak, the revenue you will get from taxes actually begins to go down, not up, as you raise taxes. One example of this was seen in 1929 when Congress passed the Hawley-Smoot Tariff Bill, in which they raised the tariff rate from 12.5% to 19.8%, but the revenue went down from $512 million to $251 million.

The hump on the laffer curve is located at approximately 33%, which is far less than the current top bracket in the U.S., which is 39.6%. This means that if we lowered the top tax rate, revenue would actually go up. One example of this happening was in the 1980's when President Reagan lowered the top tax rate from 70% to 50%, and revenues that came from the rich went up from $22 billion to $49 billion. To explain the hump on the laffer curve more simply, no matter what your political affiliation is, you do not want tax rates to exceed 33%, otherwise the government will begin to take in less money.

Now, with that being said, you may be wondering whether or not the rich "pay their fair share". Most economists and people agree that the rich category begins when you reach the top 10% of earners, or an annual salary of about $150,000. Of course, some people make more than $150,000, and there are some who make billions of dollars, but the amount of people that do is very small. Now, a fair system would be a system in which the group of people who earns 10% of the income pays 10% of the total taxes, and so on. However, the top 10% of income earners pay a tremendous 71% of the total taxes, but only make 43% of the total income. If anything, the rich, or the top 10%, are paying far more than their "fair share". On the contrary, those who make $50,200 or less, or 50% of all earners, earned 11% of the income but paid a mere 3% of the total taxes.

Now, this system may be the fairest, but it definitely wouldn't be easy to enact, and may actually be a more complex tax system. Instead, I support a 12.5% flat tax with no deductions. This tax would only apply to those who make above $88,100. Those who make any less will pay no federal income tax. This plan, according to the Tax Foundation, will create over 4,500,000 jobs, and increase incomes by at least 14%.

The only tax I have forgot about is payroll taxes. I won't edit payroll taxes, although I will phase out social security for future generations, and replace it with retirement saving laws. Anyways, many liberals argue that the payroll taxes affect lower earners more than higher earners. Firstly, it is wrong to call the payroll tax a tax. It is more of an insurance payment that guarantees you get the benefits of social security and medicare when you retire. Also, the benefits you can get from social security are capped, but the taxes aren't. This means that the payroll taxes paid by higher income earners help pay for the social security benefits that lower earners will get when they retire.

Like I said earlier, the highest federal income tax rate is 39.6%, but if you include state taxes, high income earners in states like California and New York will pay over 50% of their income into taxes, and this is just the taxes that come out of their paycheck. We also have far too many other taxes in the U.S. as well, and high income earners must pay those as well. Do you think that is fair? Someone paying most of their salary to the government? We've already learned that this high level of taxation is causing a decline in revenue, and raising it any more will only decrease revenue even more.

Now, I'm not calling for sales for the rich, or anyone in the top 10%, and I don't want to increase the struggles of lower income earners, which is why under my plan, the lowest half of earners wouldn't pay any taxes. But if you say that the rich, however you want to define the rich, do not pay their fair share, you are extremely wrong.

Finally, it is a fact that when tax rates are very high, investment and risk taking by entrepreneurs, and therefore job creation, drastically go down. When this happens, it's the poor who are hurt, not the rich. It may feel like a good thing to take away more money from the rich via taxation, but it definitely doesn't do good, and it surely is not fair.

If you go back in time and look at the American revolution, it was a revolt against taxation. Now we are taxed to live. This tax system isn't only bad because it takes money out of your pocket, but it also hurts the economy. It also takes trust out of the very government that is taxing us. If you have a bunch of loopholes or lawyers, you can get around the system and pay little to nothing. This isn't out of greed, they just take the deductions they are entitled to, at least under current law. They shouldn't get those deductions in the first place, but you or I would do the same if we could.

Nothing shows how bad our tax system has become better than the federal income tax code. This tax code is 74,608 pages, and is more than 10,000,000 words. This is 5 times the amount of words that are in the largest book ever written.

Like I said before, the taxes themselves aren't the only problem. There is also something called the cost of compliance, which is the amount of time, money, and effort that has been lost filing taxes. It is estimated that for the federal income tax alone, which is paid by individuals, approximately $100 billion is lost each year. However, if you include all taxes collected by the federal government, this number reaches $409 billion, according to the tax foundation. In other words, if we simplified the whole tax system, we would unleash an additional 2.27% GDP growth each year. This is more than the economy grew in total last year, and remember, this is additional growth. This is a lot of money that can be used in a lot of better ways, like creating new products, more product, new services, and more advancements.

It's obvious that this system needs reformation, but how we should change it has varying opinions. However, the best proposal for the federal income tax is a 12.5% flat tax, with no deductions, that applies to those who make $80,100 and above. This would dramatically simplify the tax code, something that is much needed. Under this plan, there would be about $200 billion in tax cuts each year, and the majority of Americans will be at a 0% tax bracket from the 10%-25% they currently pay. Also, as I said earlier, this plan would create over 4,500,000 jobs and increase incomes by at least 14%. Also, the rich actually will pay more in taxes. This happened in 1981 when Ronald Reagan lowered the top tax rate from 70% to 50%. Within 7 years of Reagan's plan, the top 1% paid 28% of the total taxes, up from the 18% of total taxes they paid before.

The federal income tax however isn't the only tax that needs reformation. Taxation at any level is a form of legalized theft, but right now, due to the tremendous size of the government, taxation is necessary. I'd like to shrink the government but we can't shrink it over night. Anyways, the corporate income tax is the tax I am referring to, and it should cease to exist. It draws in a mere $340 billion annually, a figure that, for the amount of damage it has caused our country, is laughable.

Firstly, if I were president, I would be the best in U.S. history for jobs. Most corporations don't pay their taxes anyways, so if the taxes are ineffective, why have them? Also, the taxes are always avoidable. Even if we still had the corporate income tax, and we eliminated loopholes or raised the rates, as liberals propose, corporations would merely move overseas. The biggest threat is China, but Mexico is up there too. Ireland however has one of the lowest rates in the world at 12.5%. The largest company in the world, Apple, paid a mere 0.005% tax rate there. Corporations will always find a way around it, and as I will continuously say, this isn't out of greed, but rather the fact they legally can. You would take these deductions too, if you could. If you deny it, you are being delusional, imagine if you could pay a 0.005% tax rate. You'd do it.

Secondly, the corporate income tax disproportionately hurts small businesses more than large businesses. Many small companies or businesses pay the extremely large 35% corporate income tax, and just like with the income tax, this is because they don't have schemes and expensive lawyers on their hands. However, if they did have those schemes and lawyers, they would avoid paying as much tax as they could. Small businesses employ 56.1 million Americans, the last thing we want to do is hurt that sector. We don't want to hurt any businesses, we want them all to grow, but we want them to grow here. Growth would be amazing if the corporate tax rate was eliminated. It is estimated that the stock market would go up at least 18.9% if this occurred. If the stock market, and therefore the value of stocks, goes up, everyone benefits. It is also estimated that wages would increase 12% (along with another 14% from my tax plan), on average, with this plan. This, along with the fact the economy would grow, shows that ending the corporate income tax not only benefits corporations and America as a whole, but it also benefits we the people.

We would attract every single business around the world by eliminating the corporate tax rate, and if other countries would like to compete with us, they must also lower the corporate tax rate, and therefore lower revenue. If real wages, GDP, and investment rise, so will revenue from other taxation, so we won't really lose very much revenue whatsoever.

Finally, the elimination of the corporate tax rate may provide an incentive to companies to bring their estimated $2.1 trillion offshore into the country. This would cause an 11% GDP growth, in addition to the 2.27% GDP increase that would occur due to the 10% flat tax system, and the elimination of the corporate income tax, which would give provide an additional 1.93% annual GDP increase. In other words, there would be an 11% GDP increase during the first year all this was enacted. The 1.93% from the corporate income tax elimination and 2.27% from the flat tax implementation would be annual, so there would be at least a 4.2% GDP increase every year after the first. Ex President Barack Obama couldn't get a single year of 3%.

To summarize, I would compromise on the federal income tax by not taxing those who make $80,100 or less annually, and would have a 12.5% flat tax on those who make more than that. I however offer no compromise for the corporate income tax. There is no compromising there, it must be eliminated. If I had the power to, I would also offer the legalization of marijuana and online gambling nationwide, and would tax those as well, but almost everyone agrees with that.

Most economists don't like the corporate income tax, as it reduces productivity, and is an additional tax on money that will be taxed in the future. If corporations raised the salary of even just their top executives, revenue would increase on the federal income tax level. Also, being pro business doesn't mean that you aren't against the elite. Businesses are the ones who create jobs, not the government. If you attack businesses, you are essentially attacking the economy. If you attack business executives and elitists who actually run some things, you are essentially attacking the power the hold. Also, the elimination of the corporate income tax would be step one in the total elimination of taxation as we know it. All in all, we must end the corporate income tax and must simplify the federal income tax system. Almost every economist agrees that at least part of the corporate income tax is paid by employees some way or another. It's time to put more money into the pockets of we the people and grow our economy, and this is how we can do it, and do it successfully.

Chapter Three
Capitalism Vs Socialism

"The inherent vice of capitalism is the unequal sharing of blessings. The inherent virtue of Socialism is the equal sharing of miseries."
-Winston Churchill

Nobody disagrees with the fact that all economic systems show the self concern about human beings. However, only the system of capitalism creates a group of people called entrepreneurs who literally have no other option than to care about the needs and desires for others. These "others" are the people that they are serving, also known as their customers. Entrepreneurs, despite what others wrongfully believe, must actually reject greed.

Firstly, responding to other people, which is exactly what entrepreneurs do, is the opposite of greed. Entrepreneurs must also collaborate with others, or build teams, to achieve their goals. Also, when entrepreneurs design goods and services, they must focus on the needs of others, not their own needs. This also is the opposite of greed.

In other words, profits are a way of measuring how well entrepreneurs or companies have served we the people. Under capitalism, the only way a business can prosper is if customers voluntarily trade for what they have to offer. Also, the only way a business can grow is if they improve the products or services they offer us. If an entrepreneur or business puts his interests over the interest of the customers, his business will fail. That's the beauty of a free market. We the people have control of the success of companies or organizations. Therefore, capitalism, in the end, is a competition of giving. Of course self interest is partially involved, why would anyone go out of their way to do something if they got nothing in return? However, the genius of capitalism, and capitalism only, is that it channels self interest into selflessness. The only way entrepreneurs or companies are able to help themselves is if they help others. In business, success is far from guaranteed. 50%

of all start-up businesses fail in 4 years or less. Those courageous people, who are the heart of capitalism, and who give us innovation and benefits, should be celebrated, not shunned. Selflessness is the only reason capitalism exists, and why capitalism works best for all.

Now that I have explained to you why capitalism works, you may be wondering whether or not capitalism is moral. Many people, especially millennials, believe that free market capitalism is selfish and immoral. They claim that the whole system is about greed and a thirst for money and for power. They also claim that it helps the rich and hurts the poor. They however are very wrong.

Free market capitalism is not only superior to any other economic system, but it is also morally superior to any other economic system as well. Here's how: the free market requires voluntary actions between people. There is no interfering or threatening. In the free market, if you want something from someone, you have to do something for them. For example, let's say that you mowed my lawn, and in exchange for your services, I paid you $20. What does that $20 actually mean? Well, it means that whenever you go to the store and ask for product, in response the store will essentially say that there are a lot of people that must be paid in order for that product to get to you. They then will ask for proof of your service, or money, in exchange for the goods or services that they provide. Think of money as proof of performance.

Liberals sometimes accuse free market capitalism of not being moral because it's a "zero-sum game" where if one person wins, someone else has to lose, just like poker. However, capitalism is nothing of the sort. If you do something good for me, such as give me product or groceries from a store, then i'll do something good for you, or give you money. I am better off because I value the products over the money, and the store is better off because they value the money over the products. It's a win-win.

Now that I have explained support for capitalism, let's look at the alternatives to capitalism. The most popular alternative to capitalism is socialism. Polls suggest that about 35% of Americans have a positive view of socialism. This is deeply alarming. Let me explain why.

In our world, more and more people are believing that capitalism, with the free market and profit motives, is based on selfishness and creates even more selfishness. More and more people are also believing that socialism is based on selflessness and produces selflessness. However, as I said earlier, the truth is the opposite. Whatever the intentions of socialism are, socialism produces far more selfish people, and a far more selfish society than capitalism does. Once this selfishness caused by socialism catches on, it's basically impossible to undo.

Before I go on, let me tell you a little story. Back in 2010, ex President Barack Obama gave a speech at George Mason University where he spoke to a large amount of college students. At one point in his speech, he stated that young people will now be able to stay on their parents health insurance plan until they turn 26. I have never seen a more positive reaction to a statement in my life. He could have said that the cure for cancer was just discovered, and the reaction would have been the same, possibly even less of an applause. I however still question what these people were happy about. The fact that they can remain dependent upon their parents until they turn 26 should appear to a young person as degrading, rather than liberating.

Throughout U.S. history, the goal of young people was to become a mature adult, and it worked. This all starts by becoming independent from their parents. However, socialism and welfare destroy this goal. Now, throughout the U.S., it is becoming more and more popular for people to live with their parents well into their 30's, and often beyond, and why not? In the welfare state, you no longer need to take care of yourself. Why? Well, because the government will be there for you. Therefore, socialism enables and creates people whose preoccupations become more and more selfish. They begin to ask how many benefits they will receive from the government, whether or not the government will pay for their higher education, whether or not the government will pay for their healthcare, when the youngest age that they can retire and collect pensions from the government is, how much paid vacation time can they get, how many days can they call in sick yet still get paid, how many days of paid maternity or paternity leave can they get, and much much more. The list gets longer as we continue to elect liberals. Liberals also make all of these forms of welfare a "right".

However, we are not done yet. There are even more problems with socialism. These entitlements or forms of welfare create people who lack the most important characteristic trait in humans: gratitude. It is impossible to be happy if you are not grateful, and it is impossible to be a good person if you are not grateful. That's why we are always raised to say thank you. However, socialism undoes this, after all, why would a person be grateful for receiving something they are entitled to? Who would be grateful for receiving their rights? So instead of thank you, the person raised in the welfare state, or socialism, is taught to ask what more they are entitled to, yet the left still insists that it is capitalism and the free market, not socialism, that creates selfish people. The truth however is that capitalism and the free market produce far less selfish people than socialism does. Teaching people to work hard and take care of themselves, as well as others, and teaching them that they should earn what they receive, produces less selfish rather than more selfish people. Capitalism teaches people to work more, which is the only way to success. Socialism teaches people to demand more. Which attitude do you think is best for our society?

Now, after all this, I have one question left: why isn't communism and socialism hated as much as nazism? When people describe evil regimes, why do they use the terms naxi or fascist, but never communist? Given the huge amount of suffering communism has caused, why is communist so much less a term of hatred than nazi? I don't support a single thing the nazis did, but communists did practically the same thing as them, and therefore should be hated as well. Communism has killed over 70 million people in China, more than 20 million people in the Soviet Union, about 5 million Ukrainians, and almost 1 in 3 Cambodians. Communists also enslaved whole nations such as Russia, Vietnam, China, North Korea, parts of eastern Europe, Cuba, and a lot of central Asia. Communism has ruined the lives of over 1 billion people, so I ask again, why doesn't communism have the same evil response that nazism gets?

Well, I think one of the reasons this is true is because communism has a lot of misconceptions. More and more young people are flocking to the idea of communism. Both the right and the left condone nazism, but the left, and i'm talking about the usual liberals, not Kennedy or Truman, have never condoned communism. Also, since the left dominates universities across the country, practically nobody teaches communism's horrible history.

I also think that people are beginning to support communism more because it has nice sounding theories, but nazism doesn't. However, as I said earlier, these theories are nowhere near the realities of communism or socialism. Many people dismiss the true evils of communism as "not true communism", but this isn't true either. Also, Germans have spoken about the evils of nazism, they have taken responsibility for them, and they apologized for them. Russia, however, has done nothing of the sort in regards to Stalin's and Lenin's evil actions. Lenin, the Soviet founder of communism, is still supported by many in Russia. In regards to Stalin, the University of London says it correctly: "People still deny, by assertion or implication, Stalin's holocaust." China hasn't done anything either regarding the greatest mass murder and enslaver of all: Mao Zedong. Mao is still widely supported in China, hell, they have him on every single currency note. Until Russia, and China, and Vietnam, and Cuba, and North Korea condemn the evils of communism, people will still not condone communism's evils, because they simply don't know about them.

Finally, to all of those who claim they support "democratic socialism", you are still supporting the very same socialism that has ruined the lives of every Venezuelan, one of the most resource rich countries in the world. As I've said before, I am a compromiser and a deal maker. However, with that being said, there is no compromising in this case. You can't go 50/50 on economic systems, and if you did, a collapse would be inevitable.

Chapter Four
Income Inequality

"There can be no liberty unless there is
economic liberty." -Margaret Thatcher

In the U.S., there has been a lot said about
income inequality. People complain about how
unfair it is that some people are rich and some
people aren't. There however is only one
problem with these complaints: they are wrong.
Income inequality is actually a good thing, only
when it is the product of a free market
economy, and my life, as well as yours, proves
this.

An economy is made up of millions of people
making choices about their own individual
lives, such as where they want to work, what
they want to buy, etc. You are one of those

people. In the U.S., you are free to go down a path in life that you believe is best for you, and therefore best suits what you are good at. You may be good at teaching, or making music, or banking, or many different things. Whatever your path is, the freedom of this helps make life good and meaningful. This choice of ambition is also an example of inequality. This is because we all have different talents and different ambitions. This however is OK because, as I stated before, we can take opportunities in the free market that distinguish us from others by allowing us to pursue what we are personally best at.

If you find what you are best at, and you work hard, you will likely have tremendous success and therefore will make a large sum of money. If you are a great athlete as an example, I will buy a ticket to watch you perform. If you are a good investor, I will give you some of my money for you to invest. As long as we the people have the freedom to determine our own personal destiny, we will have the chance to reach our full potential. Your full potential is achieving success, however you want to define it as. However, what if someone, lets say the government, told you that your success had limits and there was a ceiling to which you can not rise? I highly doubt that you would celebrate. This is called forced equality, and forced equality means that people have less of an opportunity to pursue what they personally excel at. This is what communism and socialism does, but i've already explained that. To quote the great Milton Friedman, "A society that puts equality before freedom will get neither. A society that puts freedom before equality will get a high degree of both."

Now, with all that being said, what about the growing gap that exists between the top 1% and the bottom 99%? You may be asking, isn't that a bad thing? Well, the answer again is no. Here's why. In the free market, people become rich by creating what the rich enjoy today into something that everyone can enjoy in the future. Think of the rich as test buyers. For example, look at the cell phone. Nowadays, basically everyone has one. According to Pew Research, 95% of adults have a cell phone in America. However, it didn't used to be this way. Additionally, when the first phone came out in 1983, it was the size of a brick and had horrible service and battery life. The price for this brick was $4,000. However, if no rich person had bought that $4,000 brick phone, no rich person or company would have issued the phones, and there wouldn't be $40 phones today. Another example is with computers. In the 1960s, the price of a computer was well over $1,000,000. This again is very different today. Because of billionaires like Michael Dell, we have highly advanced computers that cost a couple hundred dollars. Again, if no rich person had bought the million dollar computer in the 1960s, no rich person or company would have issued them, and cheap computers wouldn't exist today. One final example is the TV. Flat screen TVs used to cost upwards of $8,000, and therefore only the rich could buy them. Nowadays, however, practically every home has a flat screen TV, and it comes at a much cheaper price, and in much better quality.

In free market capitalism, rarity or exclusivity turns into abundance. What was once only available to the elite and upper class soon becomes available to virtually everyone, and products become improved at the same time. Wealth inequality, or income inequality, is a key factor in allowing this to happen. Instead of being mad at the wealthy because they have more money than us, we should be happy and grateful for the free market, which allows them to improve the lives of millions of people, and gives millions of other people the opportunity to do the same. Income inequality may seem bad at first, and I understand why, but when you take a closer look at it, you realize it's a good thing. Income inequality ensures innovation exists in our society. That sounds great to me.

Chapter Five
Regulation

"Those who refuse to learn from history are condemned to repeat it." -George Santayana

---

Government regulations and rules sometimes help equalize things for businesses. However, in many cases, unelected government officials and regulations can hurt businesses, and often times they don't even hurt the businesses they are trying to target. Most of the times, small businesses that are creating jobs for we the people are hurt the most. Most of the time, new rules coming out of Washington D.C. hurt franchised businesses the most.

When it comes to ownership of a business, franchisee and franchisor are two words that are often thrown around. A franchisor is like Mcdonald's. They own the brand and they license it to other people who typically own one or two stores. There are thousands of franchisors in many different industries across the U.S.

As of right now, if you would like to open a franchised restaurant, store, or whatever, you must sign a deal with the franchisor, which has the rights to the name and business model. The franchisee buys those rights, and ensures he will follow certain standards the franchisor makes.

However, the franchisee is a separate business that decides who to hire, how many people to hire, how much they will pay workers, what benefits they will offer, etc. This system of franchisees and franchisors has worked out great for America. This system supports over 770,000 small businesses and over 18 million jobs.

Right now, there is a threat to this great system. As you probably know, the federal government has a tendency to get involved in places it doesn't need to and shouldn't be involved in. The National Labor Relations Board wants to change the relationship between the franchisee and franchisor, a policy that would be detrimental to small business and workers. Their plan is to make the larger company (franchisor) and the smaller company (franchisee) equally responsible for complaints and other legal problems.

If the National Labor Relations Board succeeds in it's goal, there will be far less small businesses and the jobs that go along with them. This is because franchisors will be a lot more weary about giving inexperienced people a chance to open up a franchise, after all, why would they want to be in a relationship where they don't get to make the decisions, but they are responsible for those decisions? Also, franchisees didn't give up their savings to find out they are essentially working for the franchisor. In the end, this new plan would be detrimental to small businesses, and this is just one of the many examples of hurtful regulation.

Another example of hurtful regulation is at the gas station. Americans love to drive. We love driving so much that in the U.S., about 11 billion miles are driven each day. This is almost

40 miles per person. However, it isn't very cheap to drive, especially when you take into account taxes and fees.

For example, look at gas prices. In Pennsylvania, for every $50 spent on gas, about $10 is paid in taxes. The federal gas tax, which is applicable in all states, is 18.4 cents per gallon, and state gas taxes average out to 8.6 cents per gallon. In other words, on average, you are paying 27 cents per gallon on gas taxes. However, in 5 states, the gas tax surpasses 40 cents per gallon. This number is insanely high, and I think there should be no gas taxes whatsoever and I also believe that oil should be nationalized, but I'll explain more later.

Anyways, the gas taxes can cause lots of pain to your wallet. Each year, on average, about $177 is paid in gas taxes, according to *The Motley Fool.* This is enough to buy another 75 gallons of gas per year. I would have no problem with the government taking this money if the government was efficient and put the money to good use. However, the government doesn't know the word efficient and therefore can not function as it should.

A recent proposal was made by the Obama administration to place a $10 tax on each barrel of oil. This new tax would cost consumers about 24 cents per gallon, in addition to the 18.4 cents already in place, and the 8.4 cents that is charged on average by states. This would make the new average tax 51 cents per gallon, and this would be horrible for all. It would not only raise gas prices, which are already far too high, but this proposal would also cause job loss and a lower GDP. It is estimated that this proposal would result in the loss of 137,000 full time jobs as well as a $50 billion decrease in GDP, or a 0.27% decrease, something we definitely don't need. I guess our elected officials would rather see China surpass us economically, which is set to happen in 2022.

The government can not run the economy. The economy can only thrive with a smaller government that supports businesses, usually small. When the government gets involved in places that it shouldn't, the country becomes weaker. The stronger the country, the weaker the government. Any person, liberal or conservative, should be against regulation that hurts businesses, and there are lots of examples of hurtful regulations.

Chapter Six
Healthcare

"In politics, nothing happens by accident. If it happens, you can bet it was planned that way."
-Franklin Roosevelt

To start this off, let me just state that the U.S. has already tried a single payer system: and it failed. Let me also ask any potential liberals out there this question: If healthcare is a right and therefore the government should pay for it, should the government pay for my guns too? Additionally, the government has no place in healthcare. The Constitution isn't outdated as some state, it is just as relevant today as it was when it was written. In the Constitution, the federal government has 30 enumerated powers. All other powers are given to the states. The founding fathers knew that new issues would come up as the country aged, so they made it possible to make amendments. However, no amendment has been made regarding healthcare. Therefore, healthcare is an issue that should be left to the states. I'd possibly be open to giving the states money to spend on healthcare, but as of right now, it is a state's issue. If the law changed, I may disagree with it, but I would respect it. Until an amendment is passed, the federal government needs to step out of healthcare. The only exceptions should be the VA and Medicare, but Medicare should only be given to those who have put money into it. All future generations shouldn't pay into that failed system.

Many liberals believe that a government run healthcare system, just like the one in Canada, would work. However, we already tried a single payer system, and it has failed. Firstly, look at our veterans. They have had government run healthcare for ages.

The VA runs the largest healthcare and hospital system within the U.S. The VA has over 340,000 employees as well. It also has a budget of over $180 billion. The VA runs over

150 hospitals as well as over 1,400 community clinics based all across the country. Everyone who works for the VA is working for the government. The VA has over 7,000,000 people that it ensures. The VA is an example of a single payer system, and it is an example of a failure.

For the past couple of decades, the VA has been a failure. It has been so inefficient and has resulted in far too many deaths of the greatest people in our country. Many horrible stories about the VA began coming up around 2014. It started in Arizona where it was realized that over 1,700 veterans waited, on average, 115 days just to get an initial appointment. According to VA policy, the wait time should be no longer than 14 days. Additionally, the VA then lied about what happened and released fake wait lists.

This failure of a single payer system goes far beyond Arizona. In Colorado, VA clerks were told to fake records to make it seem as though VA doctors we're seeing even more patients than they were. In South Carolina, the failure in treatment resulted in the death of multiple veterans. Additionally, the VA there had almost

4,000 backlogged, or built up, appointments, even though they got a $1 million grant that was given to them to reduce delays. Finally, in Pennsylvania, there were many cases of legionnaires disease. Additionally, officials knew about the disease's presence for over 1 year before the outbreak. 6 veterans died because of this.

Even the Obama administration's deputy chief of staff said that VA health care has a "corrosive culture" with "significant and systemic failures". Congress's response to this whole situation was to spend more money, not make the VA efficient. You can throw as much money as you want at a trashcan, but the trashcan still won't perform any better. The budget of the VA has practically doubled since 2009. Additionally, the VA has hired about 100,000 people over the past 10 years. Wait times have also gone up too. Finally, and this is the worst part, not one person was punished for the wait list scandal at the VA.

The solution to this mess isn't a larger government or more money. Instead, the solution is more competition and effectiveness. If veterans were given HSA's, and we made deposits into them, the veterans would control their own healthcare. Additionally, the HSA's would not be taxed, and the VA would be forced to compete for the business of the veteran, and therefore prices will drop. Much better care comes out from this as patients would now be treated as customers, not just a name on a list.

Until this happens, veterans will be strangled by the far too large government who believes they can run everything. The fact that the government can't effectively run healthcare, or anything for that matter, likely explains why 14 million, or ⅔ of veterans, don't use the VA. It also explains why those who do use the VA get approximately 75% of their care outside of the VA, despite higher costs. This is because it is a failure. Anyone who can afford not to use the VA doesn't use the VA. This is why there can't be a single payer system.

My plan, which removes the government from health insurance, gives each veteran a $4,000 HSA, or $333.33 each month to spend. This is an increase from the current $3,230 per veteran spending, annually. This all in all would increase the VA's annual budget for health care to $87.33 billion from $70.7 billion. Not only that, but the quality of care would drastically go up, for once, with increased funding. This plan no longer hurts veterans, and would end the horrible single payer system at the VA.

Chapter Seven
Abortion

"Peace, commerce, and honest friendship, with all nations-entangling alliances with none."
-Thomas Jefferson

One of the most emotional and divided subjects in America is abortion. According to Gallup, 46% of Americans identify as pro life while 47% identify as pro choice. This is a practical split. However, instead of explaining whether or not abortion should be legal or illegal, I will explain why abortion is immoral.

Let me first ask this question: Does the fetus have any value or any rights? Those who claim that the fetus has no rights also claim that the fetus is not a person. It is a scientific fact that a human fetus is indeed human life. However, even if you believe that the fetus is not a person, it doesn't mean that it has no value or no rights. There are many living things that are not human but have both value as well as rights. Some of these living things are dogs or cats. A living thing doesn't have to be a person in order to have rights and value.

Now, with all that being said, what about the right of the mother? The right I am referring to is the right of the mother to end her fetus's life under any reasoning or any circumstances she wants. Additionally, in 9 states, as well as Washington D.C., there is no limit to the time in the mother's pregnancy in which she can get an abortion. Is that moral? The only way it could be moral is if the human fetus had no value.

However, in almost every case, people believe the fetus has practically infinite value, as well as an absolute right to live. This belief comes when the mother wants to give birth. Only then does society and the legal system regard the fetus as so valuable that if someone were to kill it, they would be charged with homicide. It is only if a pregnant women does not want to give birth that about half of the people think of the fetus as worthless. Does that make sense? I don't think it does. Either a human fetus has worth, or it doesn't. On what moral grounds can the mother alone decide the value of a fetus? We don't do that with newborn children. It is society, not the mother or the father, that says if a newborn child has value and a right to live. Why should that be different prior to a human being born? Why does one person get to decide if a being has a right to live?

What about the right women have to control their body? Well, it is correct that a woman has the absolute right to control her body. However, the fetus is not her body. It is in her body, and it is a totally separate body. In reference to the fetus, nobody ever asks a pregnant women how their body is. They ask how the baby is.

Additionally, virtually everyone believes that the second the baby comes out of the womb, killing it would be murder. However, killing the baby any time before it is born is considered no more immoral than removing a tooth. How does that make sense?

Finally, aren't there at least some instances where people who consider themselves pro life would say an abortion would be wrong? For example, would it be moral to abort a female fetus just because the mother wanted a male instead? People will vary on views about the legal status of abortion, but all should agree abortion is immoral. Societies can still function if people do immoral things. It can not function if the immoral things are labeled as moral.

America's largest abortion provider, planned parenthood, repeatedly claims that abortion is only 3% of the services that they offer. It's in their annual report, on their website, and is countlessly recited by Planned Parenthood supporters. However, here is why that statistic is false. Even the liberal website *Slate* says that the 3% statistic is "the most meaningless abortion statistic ever". Additionally, the *Washington Post* fact checkers have given Planned Parenthood's 3 percent statistic 3 pinocchios, which is equivalent to a mostly false rating. They also called the statistic "misleading".

If you look at the actual numbers from Planned Parenthood's annual report, Planned

Parenthood commits over 300,000 abortions per year. In 2016, they committed 323,999 abortions. This averages to about 887 abortions per day, or 37 abortions per hour, or about one abortion every 97 seconds.

Now, if the 3% statistic is false, then how much of what Planned Parenthood does is abortion? Well, if you divide the number of abortions they provide every year, or 323,999, by the number of patients they see every year, or 2,500,000, you get 12.95%, or a little more than 1/8. That's a lot more than the 1/33 that they claim.

Additionally, Planned Parenthood commits 160 abortions for every one adoption referral, which means they have their priorities set in abortion. That's perfectly legal under current law, but it is definitely against what they claim. Planned Parenthood also often touts their PAP tests and breast exams, but they only do 0.97% of America's total PAP tests, and only 1.8% of America's breast exams. On the contrary, they commit 30.6% of America's abortions.

Since Planned Parenthood knew that they would be criticized for committing 30.6% of all abortions in America, they came up with an idea to make their abortion business seem small. To get the 3% statistic, Planned Parenthood divides the number of abortions they commit, or 323,999 by services, which they define as a "discrete clinical interaction", and they count all services equally. This means that an entire abortion, which costs $390-$1,500, will be weighed the same as a pregnancy test, which costs $10 at a store. This means that Planned Parenthood can count 9.4 million services in their calculation. If you divide 323,999 by 9.4 million, you get a little over 1/29, or about 3%.

It is very easy to see why their math is entirely misleading. Let's say that a women goes to Planned Parenthood to get an abortion. If they got a pregnancy test, an abortion, and an STI test. This means that under Planned Parenthood's math, they could say that abortion is only about 33% of what they do, even though that woman came into Planned Parenthood only because she wanted an abortion. Under these circumstances, even if 100% of patients got an abortion, Planned Parenthood could say that abortion is only about 33% of their services. You could use these calculations to change the purpose of every business. It would be as though the NFL said that because they sold 1 million drinks and there were only 256 games in the season, football is only about 0.025% of what they do.

I propose that abortions be made illegal after 12 weeks. This would give time to mother's, but would end what I call cruel abortions. At 12 weeks, a baby has all organs developed and functioning, bones are developed, and the brain is emitting electrical signals. It is cruel, as well as immoral, to kill it.

Chapter Eight
Guns

"The best way to predict the future is to create it." -Abraham Lincoln

---

For my argument for guns, let me just say that the only thing that must be fixed is stopping crazy people from having a gun. I propose a psychological test be taken by all who wish to purchase a gun. This wouldn't stop people from being able to get a gun, there will always be a black market, but it would at least make it so they can't do it so easily.

According to the FBI, in 2014, 248 people were killed by all types of rifles. That very same year, blunt objects, such as clubs and hammers, killed 435 people. I don't see any proposals for a ban on hammers. Again, the 248 people killed were killed by all types of rifles, not just "assault rifles". Yes, more people were killed by handguns, but no proposal has been successful to ban handguns.

Additionally, 1,567 people died because of knives. Why is there no proposal to ban those? In 2014, knives killed over 6 times as many people as all rifles did. In 2014, 9,967 people were killed by drunk drivers. Should we ban alcohol? Finally, each year, at least 250,000 people die due to medical errors. This means you are over 1,000 times more likely to die while potentially on Obamacare than you are to die due to a rifle. However, despite this, I have heard far more proposals for gun control than I have for the reformation of the medical industry.

When liberals talk about "common sense gun control", they likely are referring to "assault weapons". The proposal of gun control is a theory that has been around since the 1960s in America. The theory is that the less amount of guns there are, the less amount of gun crime there is.

However, for this theory to have even a chance at working, basically impossible things need to happen. A very liberal senator, Howard Metzenbaum, stated this: "If you don't ban all guns, you might as well ban none of them." However, even though there are many people calling for gun control in America, practically nobody has proposed this idea. Even if you exclude the second amendment from this debate, which defeats the argument of many liberals by itself, an all out gun ban has almost no support. Even in the two very liberal states of California and Massachusetts, proposed handgun bans failed by very large margins. In California, the proposal was defeated by a 62.8 to 37.2 margin in 1982. In Massachusetts, the proposal was defeated by a 69.21 to 30.79 margin in 1976. No real attempts have been made since then.

Recently, many liberals have looked at Australia's gun control policies as a potential model for the U.S. to reflect. So, then, let's look at Australia. In 1996, a crazy person used a semi automatic rifle to kill 34 people in

Australia. In response, the Australian government banned all semi automatic rifles and even some shotguns. The owners of about 700,000 registered guns turned their guns in. However, this was only about ¼ of the country's total of about 3 million guns.

This model would surely fail if tried in the U.S. This is because the U.S. has far more guns. The U.S. has about 325 million guns, or over 100 times more guns than there are in Australia.
Even if the plan in Australia was attempted in the U.S. and weren exactly was it did in Australia, over 200 million guns would still exist. Banning guns isn't the response we should have to horrible gun crimes. The response that we should have should be one in support of more gun ownership. The criminals will always find a way to get a gun, even if you ban them. The important thing is that good people have guns to defend themselves. Saying that we don't need guns because we have the police is like saying we don't need fire extinguishers because we have the fire department. Not only is there a need for those guns, but people have a right to those guns. I put aside the second amendment for my

argument earlier, but in reality, you can never put aside the Constitution, which is the supreme law of the land. The second amendment isn't outdated, and even if it was, that doesn't make it invalid. The only way to make an amendment invalid is through another amendment, and that is yet to happen. Finally, most people today are against a ban on assault rifles. According to Gallup, 61% are against the ban while 36% are for it. The only thing that should be done is a psychological test to purchase any gun, but no bans.

Chapter Nine
Climate Change

"One man with courage makes a majority."
-Andrew Jackson

Before I get into the many many details here, let me first debunk the "97% of climate scientists agree" claim. That claim is false. If you gathered every single climate scientist on Earth and asked them for what they thought about the subject, I guarantee you that the number of people that agree wouldn't be 97%. I believe it will be lower, but who knows, maybe it will be higher. However, the number would be very different than is constantly claimed.

The claim made most often by liberals on climate change is that "97% of climate scientists agree that climate change is real", or something along that line. Most people have heard that statement made hundreds of times. It may seem like a compelling argument, but it is a very illogical statement. Let me explain how through an example involving vaccines. Let's say that an anti vaccine person comes up to you san states "97% of doctors believe that the side effects vaccines have on people are real." Your response would first likely be to show sources, but i'll get to the source of this argument later. However, after that, you would likely claim that the benefits of vaccines drastically outweigh the supposed side effects. When you say that 97% of doctors believe that vaccine side effects on people are real without stating the benefits vaccines offer, the dangers that are introduced are being introduced out of context. When people make the 97% of scientists claim on climate change, they are doing the same thing. They don't list the many many benefits that fossil fuels, and other things that emit carbon have.

Yes, using fossil fuels has a side effect, it increases the amount of carbon monoxide within our atmosphere. However, there is an upside to this. Fossil fuels are a very cheap, plentiful, and reliable source of energy, and they make our modern life possible. Fossil fuels also achieve this on a scale no other energy source can achieve. I'll add on to this later.

Another problem with the 97% claim is that never once is the meaning nor magnitude of the phrase "climate change" defined. This climate change that climate scientists "agree" on could be a slow warming, or a catastrophic warming. If one scientist believed that the warming was slow and another scientist believed that the warming was fast, that means they don't agree. However, in this case, both of them would be counted down equally. Yes, they both agree that climate change exists, but to count both of them equally is very misleading.

In 2014, former Secretary of State, John Kerry, mislead many many people when is manipulated the 97% statistic. He stated "97 percent of climate scientists have confirmed that climate change is happening, and that human activity is responsible." Later, in the exact same speech, he claimed "scientists agree that the world as we know it will change, and it will change dramatically for the worse." However, 97% of climate scientists never said anything about that.

If climate scientists didn't say what John Kerry claimed, then what did they say? Well, it turns out they they didn't say anything about cataclysmic climate change. The study that is rooted in the 97% claim comes from a study done by John Cook. His conclusion of his own survey states "Cook et al. found that over 97 percent of papers surveyed endorsed the view that the Earth is warming up, and human emissions of greenhouse gases are the main cause." Main cause means the majority, or more than half. However, the vast majority of papers surveyed didn't say that human beings were the main cause. As a matter of fact, another study found that less than 2% of those paper's surveyed actually said that. Additionally, many other scientists who had their papers included stated "Cook survey included 10 of my 122 eligible papers. 5/10 were rated incorrectly. 4/5 were rated as endorse rather than neutral.", "That is not an accurate representation of my paper . . .", "Nope . . . it is not an accurate representation.", and even "Cook et al. (2013) is based on a strawman argument . . ."

So, if 97% of scientists don't agree, how did Cook get to 97%? Well, first, he added papers that said that there was man made warming, but didn't say how much. Remember, he cited all of those surveys that didn't say how much man made warming there was when he stated man made warming was the "main cause". Then, he added papers that never said there was man made warming, but he claimed that it was implied. Cook, and researchers like him, have failed we the people to accurately report on what is out there. Politicians and media have also failed us as they blindly repeated that statistic. Finally, Cook's research, and practically any other research done, will never be accurate. Unless we get a list of every single climate scientist in the world, as well as their position on climate change, we can not make assumptions on their views. Additionally, I question how any researcher can determine what percentage of the warming is human caused. Ask any scientist how hot the Earth would be at this very moment if it weren't for humans, and they will be unable to tell you. It's impossible to determine that. However, the Earth is indeed warming, and nobody disputes that.

Now that I have thoroughly debunked the 97 percent myth, let me show you how bad the recent deal made was. It is called the Paris Climate Agreement. Many things have been said about this agreement, which was signed by 178 countries in 2016. Laurent Fabius, the French foreign minister, called it "a historic turning point." Additionally, Gina McCarthy, the head of the EPA in the previous administration said "The Paris Agreement was an incredible achievement."

This strategy of making the agreement seem great while vaguely stating what is in the agreement is a good strategy for supporters of the agreement to take. This is because if the people knew what was actually in the agreement, they would hate it.

Before I add on to that, let's look at ex President Barack Obama's Clean Power Plan. This plan will do very little to combat climate change, or anything for that matter. Even if everything in the plan was achieved, which it won't be as, thankfully, it is getting repealed, the final effect would be a 0.015 degree decrease in global temperatures by 2100. This is equivalent to delaying warming by about 2 months. Additionally, the increase in global sea levels would differentiate by ⅓ the thickness of a dime. However, these things would be good if they came for free, but there is no such thing as a free lunch. The cost of compliance for this plan is estimated to be $479 billion by 2031.

This high cost low result plan isn't the only one of it's kind. If every single country met the promises they made during the Paris agreement, the temperature in 2100 would fall by 0.3 degrees. This is the equivalent of delaying global warming by about 4 years. Again, delaying global warming by 4 years would be a great thing if we could do it for less money. We can do far more than 4 years of delays with far less money, just not with the Paris agreement. It is estimated that the Paris agreement will cost $1 trillion per year. This means the world will spend around $100 trillion by the end of the century to maybe delay global warming by 4 years, and even that is very unlikely to occur.

Additionally, many countries signed into this agreement because our stupid leader agreed to ship money to other countries for nothing in exchange. We aren't loaning $3 billion to other countries, we are simply handing it to them. Barack Obama however had a history of doing this, as we saw when we gave $1.3 billion after our hostages were released. What happened to not negotiating with terrorists? How stupid can we be? Right now, we as a nation need that $3 billion more than ever. We owe $20 trillion.

Finally, the Paris agreement is bad for not just the government, or the next generation: it is bad for you today. A potential $154 billion and $172 billion is expected to be lost annually in GDP due to the agreement. This doesn't mean our GDP would go down, it means our growth will. Our GDP almost never goes down, it just increases very slowly. Additionally, 6.5 million U.S. jobs are expected to be lost by 2040 as a result of the Paris Agreement. That is the last thing that we need right now.

The Paris Agreement is a horrible solution to an actual problem. The right solution would be to support private green energy research and development. Nuclear energy is the best energy, but I will add on to that later. A great example of private sector green energy research and development is the Breakthrough Coalition that Bill Gates is running. There is no need for a political debate on this and there is no need to subsidize current green technologies. There however is a need for huge boosts in green energy innovation, and make sure that the government isn't behind the innovation.

Carbon emissions are on the rise, and Carbon is being emitted faster than expected. However, believe it or not, there is encouraging news that has come from the climate recently.

Yes, arctic sea ice is indeed melting faster than scientists previously thought it would, but many scientists also predicted that antarctic sea ice would decrease as well. However, Antarctic sea ice is actually increasing.

Yes, sea levels are indeed rising, but the rise is not accelerating. As a matter of fact, two recent papers suggest that the rate in which sea levels are rising is actually decreasing.

We are often told that more and more droughts are occurring than before, but a recent study done by Nature shows that there is actually a decrease in Earth's surface that has been facing droughts since the year 1982.

It is also claimed that we are facing more hurricanes and more damaging hurricanes recently than in the past. However, if you take a look at the U.S, which has the greatest statistics in the world on hurricanes, if you adjust for inflation, wealth, and population, the amount of damage done per hurricane has actually decreased since 1900. Ironically, in the UN Climate Change Conference in Lima, Peru back in 2014, countries were told that carbon emissions should be cut to avoid storms like Typhoon Hagupit, which affected the Philippines whilst the conference was taking place. 21 people were killed and over 1 million people were forced to go into shelters. However, the amount of major typhoons seen in the Western North Pacific, which is where the Philippines is located, has actually decreased since 1950.

In relation to the climate, we are usually told that everything is getting worse, but facts do not support this claim. This however does not mean that global warming isn't an issue, but what I call climate alarmism distracts us from the real issues. If we want to help out poor countries, who are the ones who are the most threatened by natural disasters, it is far less about cutting carbon emissions than it is about pulling them up from poverty. The best way to look at this is to observe the amount of deaths per million people over time due to natural disasters. In the early 1900s, about 130 people per million died due to natural disasters. Since then, there has been a 97% drop in the amount of deaths due to natural disasters per million, as today less than 4 people per million are killed by natural disasters. This dramatic decline in death is mostly due to economic development that occurred during this time period that helped bring up poor countries from poverty.

For example, if you are rich like Florida, a hurricane will cause lots of damage in terms of money, since the buildings and infrastructure there is fairly expensive, but nothing is as valuable as a human life. If a hurricane were to hit Florida tomorrow, you would see very few, if any, deaths due to the hurricane. Additionally, the economic effect would only be temporary. However, if the same exact hurricane were to hit a poorer country, like the Philippines, many people would die due to it, and the economic impact would be devastating.

Alarmists like Al Gore that support alarmism through projecting that all the ice caps will melt in 5 years, as he stated in 2009 (he was very wrong on that), are also supporting a very biased climate policy of attempting to cut carbon emissions by subsidizing solar and wind. However, as I will explain later, solar and wind are very ineffective, and a combination of all energy sources, that consists mainly of nuclear and hydro power plants, is a far better solution. According to the International Energy Organization, as of right now, a mere 0.4% of global energy consumption comes from solar and wind, combined. Additionally, with very optimistic projections about future investment in wind and solar, the International Energy Agency predicts that in 2040, a still miniscule 2.2% of the world's energy consumption will come from wind and solar energy. To put it another way, for at least the next 20 years, solar and wind energy are very expensive measures to take that will have absolutely no impact on climate change. I will get into specifics on energy later.

As I have said before, the best way to combat climate change is to invest in research and development of green energy technology to lower the current costs of solar and wind energy. Why do you think China, India, and many parts of the U.S. use coal power? It's not because they're out to get the environment. It is because it is the cheapest and most reliable form of energy (along with oil). If we brought the cost of renewables down through research and development, and made them more reliable, everyone, including India and China, would want to use them instead.

Finally, most conservatives aren't denying the fact that climate change is a thing. They merely are saying that it isn't the most important issue facing our nation at this moment, and that certainly a $100 trillion spending plan contingent on the U.S. throwing away money towards other countries isn't a good idea.

Alarmism is the left's idea of a climate policy, and it doesn't work.

Chapter Ten
The Wage Gap

"Don't expect to build up the weak by pulling down the strong." -Calvin Coolidge

---

Let me start off by this chapter by asking this: If businesses could pay women 77 cents for every dollar that they have to pay a man for the same work, why don't businesses hire just women? Don't businesses want to make as much money as they can, or are they perhaps just bad at math? Well, as I will explain, it is the many people who cite the false 77 cents for every dollar gender wage gap that are really bad at math.

The 77 cents on the dollar statistic is calculated by dividing the median earnings of all full time working women by the median earnings of all full time working men. For example, If the average income of men last year was $80,000 and the average income of women last year was $61,600, you would get a pay gap of 77 cents. However, this statistic does not reveal a gender wage gap. This is because this statistic does not look at occupation, position, education, or hours worked per week. Even a study done by the American Association of University Women, which is a feminist organization, shows that the real gender wage gap is just 6.6 cents when you take into account different choices men and women make. The key word here is choice. The small wage gap that does exist has absolutely nothing to do with paying women less, or anything to do with sexism. It has to do with different career choices that women and men make.

In 2009, the U.S. Department of Labor released a report that looked at more than 50 peer reviewed studies. Their conclusion was that the 23 cent wage gap was false. Here is their exact conclusion: "The differences in raw wages may be almost entirely the result of the individual choices being made by both male and female workers." So, if that is the cause of the wage gap, let's look at some of those different choices men and women make.

Georgetown University has created a list of the 5 highest and lowest paying majors you can take in college. They also stated on that same list the percentage of men and women who were taking those majors. The highest paying major was petroleum engineering, which was 87% male dominant. The second highest paying major was pharmaceutical sciences, which was 52% female dominant. The third highest paying major was mathematics and computer science, which was 67% male dominant. The fourth highest paying major was aerospace engineering, which was 88% male dominant. Finally, the fifth highest paying major was chemical engineering, which was 72% male dominant. Notice that women only outnumber men in one major, and it is only by 2 percent.

Next, let's look at the 5 lowest paying majors. The lowest paying college major is counseling and psychology, which is 74% female dominant. The second lowest paying major in college is early childhood education, which is 97% female dominant. The third lowest paying major is theology and religious vocations, which is 66% male dominant. The fourth lowest paying major is human services and community organization, which is 81% female dominant. Finally, the fifth lowest paying major is social work, which is 88% female dominant. In this case, it was the females, not the males, that led in 4 out of the 5 majors. This isn't sexist, it is merely factual. Women are more likely to choose lower paying majors in colleges, and that is totally fine. In America, we have a wonderful thing called free will. You could choose to do practically whatever you want, just don't go out and blame sexism on your choices.

Even if you look in the exact same career, men and women make different choices. Are these choices always made the same? Absolutely not, but according to the 2015 American Time Use survey, which was conducted by the U.S. Bureau of Labor Statistics, on average, each day, full time working men work 8.2 hours compared to full time working women who worked 7.8 hours. This may not seem like a lot at first, but the difference each day equates to 24 minutes per day, which is an extra 2 hours of work each week, or an extra full day of work, or 8 hours, each month. This means men, on average, work 96 hours more than women each year. Again, this doesn't represent every case, but it is what happens on average. This, again, is also OK. Women can choose to work however long they please, as can men.

The Department of Labor report that I was explaining earlier also stated that when everything is taken into account, the new wage gap is between 4.8 and 7%, very close to the AAUW estimate. However, one might ask, why is there any gap whatsoever? Nobody really knows, but both the AAUW, the Department of Labor agree that there are far too many factors that affect wages that no single study can take all of them into account. Of course I, along with basically everyone in America, support equality for men and women. But if that is what you would like, you need to look no further than our current society.

Chapter Eleven
Immigration

"The ballot is stronger than the bullet."
-Abraham Lincoln

Every good immigration proposal or policy has two things in common. The first thing is to take back control of the border so that we can decide who comes in. The second thing is to deal with the approximately 11 million illegal immigrants who currently reside in our country.

Let's start with the second thing that the good policies have in common. It would be best if current law was enforced and these 11 million illegals were deported, but that really isn't likely. It is feasible and would cost less than it costs in one year to the federal government to keep them here and support them, but it would still be a practically impossible task. However, we do know that it is possible to deport some illegals. It would be very easy to deport the ones who are currently in our prison, and that must be done immediately. We also must deport all illegals with any criminal record. This would result in the deportation of about 2 million illegals, and I think practically everyone would agree that must be done.

After that, we have a choice. We can either ignore the rest of the illegals, which hasn't worked, or we can give them a form of legalization. There is however still a problem with legalization. Legalizing the illegals creates an incentive for other illegals to come here illegally, rather than go come in legally. This is why a physical barrier, as well as more agents to patrol the border, are necessary, but I will get to that later.

Many of the people who oppose legalization will support it if they found out that we would be stopping future illegals from coming in, and we can do that. The best way to do that is to build a physical barrier, call it a wall, call it whatever you want. We just need a physical barrier that has a camera's, sensors, and many patrol agents. I will estimate total costs later, but barriers do work. In San Diego it worked, in Israel, it worked, even in Europe, Hungary, Macedonia, Austria, Bulgaria, Greece, Spain, and even Norway are all constructing physical barriers at their border.

In addition to approximately 2 million illegals being deported and a physical barrier (that I will explain later) being built, two other things must be done. A national e-verify system must be put in place. This would stop illegals from being able to work, even if they got passed our wall or were never deported. Secondly, we must create a fully functional visa tracking system, since about 40% of illegals in the U.S. are visa overstayers. I'd like the wall to look as good as it can, but it may look ugly. However, many things that do an effective job look ugly, just like the barriers that are made of concrete that keep people from driving into the White House.

Finally, I must discuss the legalization we should give the other 9 million illegals. We can give the illegals a choice: they can either voluntarily go back to whatever country they came from, and try to come back in legally, or they can stay here, but they will have permanent residence, not citizenship. We will not give them the right to vote, they gave that up by coming here illegally, and I think almost everyone will agree with me on that one too.

Additionally, we must end sanctuary cities. Sanctuary cities are horrible. Sanctuary cities blatantly insult the best immigrants, which are the ones who come here legally. There is no other developed country that supports illegal immigration like this. Sanctuary cities encourage people to come here illegally, and then be rewarded. That's not how it should be, we should encourage legal immigration instead.

Finally, we should create a queue system at the border, in which we evaluate who we think is best, and let them in first. For example, if someone with a college degree applies for U.S. citizenship, and someone else that has never

had a skilled job applies for citizenship, we will
accept the one with a college degree first. We
should also cap the amount of people we
accept into the U.S. at 0.2% of the U.S.
population, annually. Last year, 752,800
people were naturalized. This new law would
bring that down to 648,240. This would ensure
that the best people come into the country who
can provide the most to our country.

Illegal immigration isn't something that most
people support, I mean, it is indeed illegal.
According to Gallup, 59% of Americans worry
ether a great deal or a fair amount about illegal
immigration. It is time to take back control of
our border.

Now, it is time to look at the physical barrier.
First, lets look at the cameras. It will cost a total
of about $5,500 to both buy and install each
security camera. Each camera will be able to
look, panoramically, about 300 feet. This
means that we will need a total of about 35,000
cameras on our border. The total cost will be
about $200 million. Note that on the federal
level, illegal immigration costs $29 billion
annually, so this one time cost would be

equivalent to the cost of illegals in less than 3 days.

Now, I would like to have each agent watching 10 cameras at all times. Since each person will need to work 8 hour shifts, we will need to hire a total of 10,500 agents to watch cameras. Each agent will be paid about $95,000 per year, and the total cost will be about $1 billion annually. This is equivalent to the cost of illegals in less than 2 weeks.

Next, let's look at regular border patrol agents. Currently, there are 21,000 border patrol agents. That number need to go up to 25,000 agents. The salary of each of these agents will be doubled from $49,000 to $98,000 annually. This means the total cost will be about $2.5 billion. This is equivalent to the cost of illegals every month.

Additionally, let's look at the barrier itself. I would like for the barrier to be a 40 foot tall aluminum fence. I would also like for this barrier to be barbed wired every 5 feet (vertically). The total cost for this would be $5.4 billion, excluding the cost to install it. If we include that, the total cost will be about $10 billion, or the amount of money illegals cost every 5 months.

Finally, let's look at the cost for the drones that must be on this border. The cost to build a drone is about $64 million. I would like to have 8 drones in the sky at all times so any drone could get to any location within one hour. Since the drones will need to be switched about every day, we will need a total of 16 new drones made. The total cost will be about $1 billion. Then, we need to take into account salaries, and total cost of flying per hour. It costs about $3,600 per hour per drone to fly, which means it will cost about $250 million for 8 frones to be in the sky at all time, putting the total cost of drones at $1.25 billion, or the amount of money illegals cost us in less than 3 weeks.

All in all, these policies would give us back control of our border, which is something that we badly need. The total cost of these policies will be a one time cost of about $12 billion, and an annual cost of about $3 billion. This means that the cost of drastically improving the quality of our border is far cheaper than the cost of complying with illegal immigrants.

Chapter Twelve
Energy
"Every generation needs a revolution."
-Thomas Jefferson

Are solar and wind the answer to all of our energy problems? It may seem like so, as there is indeed a lot of sun and a lot of wind, they are free, they are clean, and there is no carbon emissions. So, then what is the problem? How come solar and wind combined provide less than 2% of the world's total energy?

To answer this question, we must understand what makes any energy source, or anything for that matter, plentiful and cheap. For anything to be plentiful and cheap, the entire process to create that thing must be plentiful and cheap. While it is true that the sun and wind are free, the process of transforming sun and wind into power on a large scale is very expensive. In fact, if you compare solar and wind energy to other energy sources, like nuclear energy and coal, wind and solar are actually fairly expensive.

The biggest problem with wind and solar is that they are weak and unreliable. These are called the dilution problem and the intermittency problem. The dillutence problem is that unlike other sources of energy, solar and wind do not provide concentrated energy, which means that lots of other materials are needed to provide the same unit of energy that a simple barrel of oil can or a simple piece of coal can. In the case of solar, those materials can be highly purified silicon, phosphorus, boron, titanium dioxide, and even more materials. All of those materials must be mined, refined, and manufactured to make a solar panel. This process isn't exactly environmentally friendly, or cheap. That process requires lots of energy. For wind, the materials are high performance compounds and rare earth metals, as well as the creation of steel and concrete.

As big of a problem as that may seem, it is nothing compared to the next problem. You likely already knew this, but the sun doesn't shine all the time, and the wind doesn't blow all the time. The only way that solar and wind could be effective on a large scale is if we could store the energy they created, so we could use it whenever we needed to. You can store oil in a barrel, or in a tank, but how do you store solar or wind power? No such mass storage system is in existence today. This is why nowhere in the world there is no real independent solar or wind power plant. All of the plants have and require a backup source, and that source is almost always fossil fuel.

Let's take a look at solar power in Germany, which is the world's leader in renewable energy. In Germany, wind varies all the time, and sometimes disappears entirely. Solar also disappears in the winter, which is when Germany needs energy the most. Therefore,

Germany, like any other country, uses a reliable source of energy when they need it. In their case, that reliable energy is coal. Additionally, despite Germany spending tens of billions of dollars in subsidies for solar and wind, coal consumption hasn't decreased. It has actually increased.

Finally, switching back and forth between resources used to generate energy is costly. In fact, utility bills in Germany have gone up so much that energy poverty has become a popular term to describe people who can't pay or can barely pay for their electric bill. If those bills do indeed go down one day, it will not be because of more government subsidies. It will be because the price of oil or coal went down. There is no such thing as a free lunch, and there is no such thing as free energy. Solar and wind are included.

The estimated cost per kilowatt hour of coal is 3.14 cents. The estimated cost per kilowatt hour of nuclear energy is 2.16 cents. The estimated cost per kilowatt hour of solar is 18.12 cents. The estimated cost per kilowatt hour of wind is 3.14 cents. This means that, compared to coal, wind is the exact same price, but as I said earlier, it isn't reliable. However, if you compare coal to solar, coal is about 6 times cheaper. However, if you compare any energy source to nuclear energy, nothing comes close. Coal and wind power are about 50% more expensive than nuclear energy. Additionally, solar is about 9 times as expensive as nuclear energy. This is why nuclear energy is the key to our country's energy revolution.

Finally, electric cars aren't as green as you think. Electric cars are powered by the electric grid, which is comprised mainly of fossil fuels in the U.S. This means that just like any other car, electric cars are powered by fossil fuels. Over the course of the lifetime of the average electric car, it will have emitted 31 metric tons of carbon. However, a similar car, the Mercedes cdi A160, will have emitted just 34 metric tons of carbon in it's lifetime. This is a 3 metric ton difference. In Europe, it currently costs $7 to cut one metric ton of carbon. This means that it only costs $21 to cut the same amount of carbon that the government offers thousands of dollars in subsidies for. This is government inefficiency, it is a waste of our money, and it has to stop.

Liberalism Debunked

Chapter Thirteen
Education

"An investment in knowledge pays the best interest." -Benjamin Franklin

---

Education is a subject America can agree on, to an extent. No matter who you are, if you are an American citizen, you should believe that all American children deserve the right to an education. I however believe that the quality of that education shouldn't be determined by your zipcode, and I am not alone. According to Gallup, 59% of Americans support school choice. If you are unfamiliar with the idea, let me explain.

School choice is the idea that students should get to go to the school that best fits their needs. It could be a private school, a public school, homeschooling, whatever. If it is best for you, no matter your zipcode, you should have the right to go to that school. Who would determine which schools are best for you? Well, the answer is both yourself and your parents. Instead of having to go to a school because it is closest to you, you will get to attend the school that is best. The funding for this will be simple. We will increase per capita spending for students, and convert that spending into vouchers, each of which worth the same amount of money. If you decide a public school is best for you, that voucher will cover your education each year entirely. If you choose to go to a nonpublic school, you essentially have a discount of thousands of dollars. The government is spending the exact same, or perhaps more to increase the quality of school, but the people get what is truly best for them, and at either an equal or cheaper price.

This is the system that works best. However, this system only works if you allow states to set their budget. Federal K-12 funding should go up, but the money should be given at a per student rate to the states. This means that you will get a larger voucher, as well as a much higher quality of education than you do currently.

Moving past school choice, but staying on the subject of K-12 education, let's examine Common Core. Only 42% of Americans support Common Core, and if trends continue, that number will continue to go down. What Common Core does is overcomplicates everything. The goals of Common Core are good, but the Common Core standards are not going to achieve the goals. Instead of confusing kids, why don't we focus on two things: teaching kids about true issues, as well as allowing room for innovation.

The world changes, and so do teaching methods. However, Common Core doesn't allow this. It stalls any improvements in teaching methods. Additionally, one of the biggest problems with schools is that you are essentially taught nothing about the real world.

You are taught how to find the hypotenuse of a triangle, but not taught about compound interest. You're taught how to solve a word problem regarding saving but not taught how to save, or the best methods of saving/investing. Hell, you aren't even taught what the Dow or Nasdaq are. You are taught about how many strawberries Steve can eat or give away, but you aren't taught how to grow any strawberries. Finally, you are not taught about the law. You were never told how to fill out a 401k. You were never told how to open a business. You were never told about any of the vast majority of our laws, and you surely won't get taught about them in a Common Core classroom. Common Core must be ended. Common Core should be replaced with very simple and obvious standards, such as math must be taught, etc, and would also add that you must be taught certain real world issues, such as taxation, the law, saving, etc, and leave the rest up to states. This is how you get the next generation to be prepared and innovative, rather than confused and unemployed.

Finally, let's look at higher education. Liberals seem to believe that community college should be offered tuition free. As a matter of fact, a little over 60% support the idea. However, it is an insanely crazy idea, especially coming from the party that claims to support lower income families (despite destroying Detroit, Chicago, and many other low income cities). Anyways, let me explain. If you made community college free, it would cost $70 billion annually. Although this number is a lot less than the $1.7 trillion annual medicare for all plan liberals support, it is still an insanely high figure to even consider.

Additionally, simply making college free for all actually benefits middle and upper income Americans more than it does poor income families. This is due to the fact that most people who attend community college exceed the federal poverty line, in many cases by a lot. Also, community college is highly ineffective, even if you end up graduating from the community college, which is something that a mere 57% do within a six year period. Also, less than one in seven Americans who attend community college will end up transferring and graduating from a better school. The average salary of the 57% who graduate community college is about $37,000. On the contrary, those who graduate from a private university earn about $45,000, on average. This is about 20% more, and much better for your long term success than a degree from a community college. Not only does this prove that there is no such thing as a free lunch, but it also proves how stupid of an idea it is to offer free college to everyone. If you would like to help lower income families, give them, and them specifically, grants to go to college, but even that is a stupid idea, as I will explain later.

Also, knowing that the government will be there with their checkbook no matter the cost, community colleges will raise costs. This is also one of the many reasons why the $70 billion annual figure is a bad estimate. This may seem like simple economics, but when you give something away for free, more people want it. When more people want something, the price goes up. That's what we have seen with the federal student loan program, which has caused the price of college to go up over 260% since 1980, which is more than double the 120% increase in the Consumer Price Index, or CPI over the same time period. The federal student loan program should be ended entirely. If it was ended, cost of college would drastically decrease, as would the national debt, over time. This is due to very simple economics, as explained earlier.

Additionally, over $1.5 trillion in student loans are still unpaid, and this number increases by over $2,500 every second. The federal government also forgives people for costing them money. There are so many ways you can get forgiven on federal student loans, and all of which are insane. If you are in debt, you are in debt. The U.S. loaned you money. You can either declare bankruptcy, and try to survive economically with that on your record, or you need to pay back your debt plus interest. You don't get to pay just a percentage of your loans just because. Putting aside the laws enacted by our horrible leaders, federal student loans are the sole reason that the cost of college is increasing at the rate it is. Ending federal student loans would allow the free market to do what it does best. Those who have worse credit will get a worse interest rate. Those who have a better one will get a better interest rate, etc. The student gets the money he needs today for college, and the government doesn't need to pay for it. It's a great solution. Plus, due to the fact colleges wouldn't be able to attract as many if they don't lower their annual cost, they will either offer more scholarships, or lower cost, but likely will do a combination of both.

If everything I just wrote in regards to education happened, our country would rank much better in terms of education, and costs would go down.

Sources

Chapter 1
The New York Times, The Right Minimum Wage: $0.00, January 14, 1987
Forbes, Instead Of $15, Or $7.25, There Should Be No Federal Minimum Wage At All, August 7, 2015
Chapter 2
The Economist, The Case For Flat Taxes, April 14, 2005
Human Events, Why A Flat Tax Is The Right Way To Go On Taxes, July 28, 2015

The New York Times, End Corporate Taxation, May 3, 2014

PBS, Why Abolishing The Corporate Income Tax Is Good For American Workers, February 17, 2014

Chapter 3

Forbes, How Capitalism Will Save Us, November 3, 2009

The New York Times, A Call For A Free Market, September 1, 2015

Harvard, The Black Book Of Communism: Crimes

Chapter 4

The Washington Post, How Income Inequality Benefits Everybody, March 25, 2015

CNBC, Income Inequality: Is It Good For Everyone?, January 8, 2013

Inside Sources, Why Income Inequality Might Actually Be A Good Thing, October 11, 2016

Chapter 5

Fortune, This Overlooked Labor Rule Could Be A Huge Drag On U.S. Businesses, May 14, 2017

Tax Foundation, What Would The Administration's $10 Oil Tax Do To The

Economy And Federal Revenue?, February 16, 2016

Chapter 6

CNN, Report: 1,700 vets not on Phoenix VA wait list, at risk of being "lost or forgotten", May 30, 2014

The Hill, WH Report Finds "Corrosive Culture" At VA, June 27, 2014

Chapter 7

Gallup, Abortion, May 4-8, 2016

The New York Times, Abortion Restrictions In States, June 18, 2013

The Washington Post, For Planned Parenthood Abortion Stats, '3 Percent' And '94 Percent' Are Both Misleading, August 12, 2015

Slate, The Most Meaningless Abortion Statistic Ever, May 7, 2013

Planned Parenthood, Annual Report, Fiscal Year 2016, 2016

Fox News, New Report: Abortions In U.S. Drop To Lowest Level Since 1974, January 18, 2017

Chapter 8

U.S. News, Medical Errors Are Third Leading Cause Of Death In The U.S., May 3, 2016

FBI, Crime In The U.S. 2014, 2014

CDC, Impaired Driving: Get The Facts, January 26, 2017

Ballotpedia, California Proposition 15

Ballotpedia, Massachusetts Prohibition Of Handguns (1976)
Business Insider, Australia's Solution To Gun Violence, June 14, 2016
Gallup, Guns, October 5-9, 2016

Chapter 9

New York Times, Kerry Implores Indonesia On Climate Change Peril, February 16, 2014
Forbes, '97% Of Climate Scientists Agree' Is 100% Wrong, January 6, 2015
Library of Economics and Liberty, 1.6%, Not 97%, Agree That Humans Are The Main Cause Of Global Warming, March 1, 2014
The Hill, EPA's Carbon Plan Isn't Environmental Policy, But Pain And Politics, August 11, 2014
Real Clear, President Obama's Clean Power Plan: All Cost, No Benefit, August 5, 2015
National Economic Research Associates, Potential Impacts Of The EPA Clean Power Plan
Lomborg, Paris climate promises will reduce temperatures by just 0.05°C in 2100
Forbes, What's The Price Tag Of Paris' Climate Summit? Don't Ask The Politicians, December 7, 2015

The New York Times, What Is the Green Climate Fund and How Much Does the U.S. Actually Pay?, June 2, 2017

The Heritage Foundation, Consequences of Paris Protocol: Devastating Economic Costs, Essentially Zero Environmental Benefits

Fortune, The U.S. Sent Another $1.3 Billion to Iran After Hostages Were Released, September 6, 2016

NASA, Antarctic Sea Ice Reaches New Maximum

Nature, Global Integrated Drought Monitoring And Prediction System, March 11, 2014

The New York Times, Philippines Pushes Developing Countries To Cut Their Emissions, December 8, 2014

Journal Of Climate, Historical Tropical Cyclone Landfalls, 2012

Chapter 10

AAUW, The Simple Truth About The Gender Pay Gap

The Huffington Post, Wage Gap Myth Exposed-By Feminists, November 4, 2012

CBS News, The Gender Pay Gap Is A Complete Myth, April 17, 2011

Forbes, Don't Buy Into The Gender Pay Gap Myth, April 12, 2016

The Huffington Post, Close The Wage Gap By Changing Your Major, June 5, 2013

Forbes, New Report: Men Work Longer Hours Than Women, June 30, 2016

Chapter 11

Wall Street Journal, Number Of Illegal Immigrants In U.S. Holds Steady At 11 Million, September 20, 2016

Gallup, In U.S, Worry About Illegal Immigration Steady, March 20, 2017

USCIS, Naturalization Fact Sheet

Wikipedia, Economic Impact Of Illegal Immigrants In The United States

Chapter 12

New Hampshire Department of Energy, Energy Cost Comparisons

NPR, Solar And Wind Energy May Be Nice, But How Can We Store It?, April 5, 2016

Energy Post, Renewables Break Records In Germany But Coal Holds On, March 24, 2016

Fortune, Germany's High Priced Energy Revolution, March 13, 2017

The Washington Post, Europe's Cap-And-Trade Program Is In Trouble. Can It Be Fixed?, April 20, 2013

Chapter 13

Gallup, Education, 2016

Harvard, Education Poll, 2016

Time, College Grad Starting Salary, May 12, 2017

Forbes, Six Reasons Why Obama's Free Community College Is A Poor Investment, January 11, 2015

Business Insider, Why A Lot Of Economists Hate The Idea Of Free Public College, March 2 ,2016

Forbes, Does Federal Student Aid Cause Tuition Increases? It Certainly Enables Them, October 8, 2015

Market Watch, Watch America's Student Loan Debt Grow $2,726 Every Second, January 30, 2016

AEI, How Much Will "Free College" Cost? New Study Suggests Colleges Respond To More Financial Aid By Increasing Tuition, February 8, 2016

Forbes, It's Well Past Time To Scrap The Federal Student Loan Program, June 26, 2013

Index

A

B

bad, 5-7
balance, 8
be, 5-6, 8-9
because, 6, 9-10
becoming, 10
before, 9
begins, 7
being, 6, 8
believe, 8
believed, 5
best, 9-10
better, 6, 10
Bono, 2, 5
book, 3, 5-6
books, 5
Budget, 8
but, 6, 8-10
buyers, 8
By, 2
by, 5-10
can, 8, 10

C

Capitalism, 4
case, 5, 9
cause, 8
certain, 6, 9
Change, 4

itself, 6

⌐

Jefferson, 6
jobs, 7-9
just, 6, 10

K

know, 7
known, 10

L

labor, 10
ladder, 7
Later, 6
Lead, 2
lead, 10
learned, 7
learning, 7
least, 7, 9
left, 5
less, 10
Let, 6
level, 7
Liberal, 1-10
liberal, 6-7
Liberalism, 5-6
liberalism, 6
Liberals, 7
liberals, 10

Liberalism Debunked

the, 3, 5-10
their, 6, 10
them, 7-8
Theodore, 7
There, 6, 9
These, 7
They, 9-10
they, 6, 9-10
thing, 9
things, 7, 10
think, 10
This, 9-10
this, 3, 5-7, 9-10
Thomas, 6
those, 3, 5, 9
three, 5
time, 5, 8-9
Times, 9
To, 1-10
to, 3, 5-10
too, 6, 8
truly, 10
Truth, 2
truth, 7
trying, 10
Two, 7
two, 10
typical, 6

Liberalism Debunked

you, 5-6, 8, 10

www.ingramcontent.com/pod-product-compliance
Lightning Source LLC
Chambersburg PA
CBHW020540290526
45786CB00002B/975